Chartered Institute for Securities & Investment Level 3 Investment Operations Certificate (IOC™)

OTC Derivatives Administration
Practice Examinations

Syllabus version 10

APPROVED WORKBOOK

BPP LEARNING MEDIA

Published August 2012

ISBN 9781 4453 9170 0

British Library Cataloguing-in-Publication Data
A catalogue record for this book
is available from the British Library

Published by

BPP Learning Media Ltd
BPP House, Aldine Place
London W12 8AA

www.bpp.com/learningmedia

Printed in the United Kingdom by Ricoh
Ricoh House, Ullswater Cresent
Coulsdon CR5 2HR

Your learning materials, published by BPP Learning Media Ltd, are printed on paper obtained from traceable, sustainable sources.

© BPP Learning Media Ltd – August 2012

All rights reserved. No part of this publication may be reproduced, stored in a retrieval system or transmitted in any form or by any means, electronic, mechanical, photocopying, recording or otherwise, without the prior written permission of BPP Learning Media.

The contents of this book are intended as a guide and not professional advice. Although every effort has been made to ensure that the contents of this book are correct at the time of going to press, BPP Learning Media, the Editor and the Author make no warranty that the information in this book is accurate or complete and accept no liability for any loss or damage suffered by any person acting or refraining from acting as a result of the material in this book.

Every effort has been made to contact the copyright holders of any material reproduced within this publication. If any have been inadvertently overlooked, BPP Learning Media will be pleased to make the appropriate credits in any subsequent reprints or editions.

A note about copyright

Dear Customer

What does the little © mean and why does it matter?

Your market-leading BPP books, course materials and e-learning materials do not write and update themselves. People write them: on their own behalf or as employees of an organisation that invests in this activity. Copyright law protects their livelihoods. It does so by creating rights over the use of the content.

Breach of copyright is a form of theft – as well being a criminal offence in some jurisdictions, it is potentially a serious beach of professional ethics.

With current technology, things might seem a bit hazy but, basically, without the express permission of BPP Learning Media:

- Photocopying our materials is a breach of copyright
- Scanning, ripcasting or conversion of our digital materials into different file formats, uploading them to facebook or e-mailing them to your friends is a breach of copyright

You can, of course, sell your books, in the form in which you have bought them – once you have finished with them. (Is this fair to your fellow students? We update for a reason.) But the e-products are sold on a single user license basis: we do not supply 'unlock' codes to people who have bought them secondhand.

And what about outside the UK? BPP Learning Media strives to make our materials available at prices students can afford by local printing arrangements, pricing policies and partnerships which are clearly listed on our website. A tiny minority ignore this and indulge in criminal activity by illegally photocopying our material or supporting organisations that do. If they act illegally and unethically in one area, can you really trust them?

Practice Examinations

Contents

Practice Examinations	Page Number	
	Questions	Answers
Practice Examination 1	3	13
Practice Examination 2	17	27
Practice Examination 3	31	41

Practice Examination 1

50 Questions in 1 Hour

1. The original development of the futures markets was most helped by
   - A Standardising the contracts to enhance liquidity
   - B Providing a location for buyers and sellers to meet
   - C Allowing international participants to trade
   - D Listing only agricultural products

2. If a forward position in an equity index contract is held to the delivery date, what happens?
   - A The seller must deliver the underlying equities to the buyer
   - B The seller must deliver the underlying equities to the exchange
   - C The seller must deliver the underlying equities to the clearing house
   - D The seller's position will be closed with a cash settlement

3. A trader can cover his market position equally well by hedging with a futures contract or an OTC trade. Why might he prefer the futures contract?
   - A Credit constraints
   - B Margin requirements
   - C Relationship development
   - D Regulatory costs

4. One of the purposes of OTC derivatives is to hedge the market risk on the underlying products. Which of the following defines the role played by a trader whose actions tend to keep the derivatives, and the cash markets in line, and thus enable the derivative to be an effective hedge?
   - A Speculator
   - B Hedger
   - C Arbitrager
   - D None of the above

5. Which of the following statements about the LIBOR fixing is false?
   - A The rates are fixed each business day
   - B The BBA is the controlling authority for the process
   - C It is used by a wide range of derivatives contracts for settlement calculations
   - D All currencies except euro are fixed

6. When is euro LIBOR fixed?

   A   At 11:00 Central European time
   B   At 11:00 London time
   C   At 11:00 New York time
   D   At the close of the European business day

7. A speculator believes that the 6-month interest rate will fall over the coming months. How might he best take advantage of this view?

   A   Buy an FRA
   B   Sell an FRA
   C   Borrow money for 6 months and buy an FRA
   D   Borrow money for 6 months and sell an FRA

8. A sells a CHF FRA to B at 1.5%. The fixing is 1.75%. Why might A have entered into the trade?

   A   He was worried that rates would rise
   B   He had a loan exposure and was protecting his position
   C   He was speculating that rates would fall below 1.5%
   D   He had bought an equivalent future and was cutting his position

9. An FRA is traded for the period 10 March to 10 April, for €1,500,000 and at 3.75%. On 8 March 1-month EURIBOR is fixed at 3.25%. What is the outcome?

   A   The seller pays € 644.03 to the buyer
   B   The buyer pays € 644.03 to the seller
   C   The buyer pays € 4830.23 to the seller
   D   The seller pays € 4830.23 to the buyer

10. Which of the following statements about an IRS is false?

    A   Both parties suffer credit exposure to the other
    B   Both parties may pay or receive settlements over the swap's life
    C   Both parties have the same underlying exposure
    D   Both parties agree on a reference rate to be used

11. Which of the following best describes delta?

    I   Delta is the likelihood of exercise
    II   Delta shows the change in the value of an option to a change in the underlying
    III Delta is the hedge ratio

    A I only
    B II and III
    C III only
    D I, II and III

12. A speculative trader believes that the yield curve, which is currently positive, will flatten. Which swap would profit from this view being correct?

    A Paying 3-month fixed rate and receiving 3-month LIBOR
    B Paying 3-month LIBOR and receiving 6-month LIBOR
    C Paying 6-month LIBOR and receiving 3-month LIBOR
    D Paying 3-month LIBOR and receiving base rate

13. A British company has won a contract to export regular shipments of goods to the USA over a five-year period. It chooses to use a currency swap to fully cover its foreign exchange exposure. Which of the following structures would most accurately meet this need?

    A Pay fixed US$, receive floating £, no principal exchanges
    B Pay fixed US$, receive fixed £, no principal exchanges
    C Pay fixed US$, receive floating £, final principal exchange only
    D Pay fixed US$, receive fixed £, final principal exchange only

14. Under the ISDA 30/360 convention, how many days are there from 17 February to 17 April in a leap year?

    A 30
    B 58
    C 59
    D 60

15. What is an 'IMM date'?

    A Any business day on which the IMM is open
    B The first available business day each month
    C The third Monday of every month
    D The third Wednesday of March, June, September and December

16. A bank has written a call option on 1,000 oz of gold. Which of the following is true?
    A The bank will profit from a rise in the price of gold
    B At expiry, the bank will exercise the option if the price of gold is high enough
    C The bank may choose to sell the gold at expiry
    D The premium may not be enough to ensure an overall profit at expiry

17. **Gamma decribes**
    A The change in the value of an option given a change in volatility
    B The change in the delta of an option given the change in the underlying
    C The change in the value of an option given a reduction in time
    D The change in the value of an option given a change in interest rates

18. **Net Present value allows risk managers to**
    A Assess the future value of a portfolio
    B Compare the values of cash-flows occurring at different future values
    C Assess the volatility of a portfolio
    D Calculate the delta of a portfolio

19. A fund manager has sold a call option on the FTSE 100 index struck at 4000 in an amount GBP 1,000 per full point for a premium of GBP 50,000. At expiry the index stands at 4200. What is the overall result for the fund manager?
    A Breakeven
    B A profit of GBP 150,000
    C A loss of GBP 150,000
    D A profit of GBP 50,000

20. The USD/JPY spot rate is 120.00. A currency trader pays USD 25,000 for a USD put option on USD 1 million with a strike of 120.00. What is his breakeven exchange rate?
    A 120.25
    B 122.50
    C 123.00
    D 117.00

21. An option is priced at 25, based on a volatility of 10%. All other things constant, if volatility rises to 11%, what will happen to the option's value?
    A The option's value will increase
    B The option's value will decrease
    C The option's value will remain unchanged
    D Not enough information is given

22. A trader is long a call on a specific government bond. Why might he have done this deal?

    I   He thinks the bond prices will rise
    II   He wants to realise the option's time value
    III He is hedging his long bond position
    IV He thinks the outlook is for lower inflation

A I and II
B II and IV
C III and IV
D I and IV

23. If you sell a call option and buy a put option on the same underlying, with the same maturity and with the same strike, what is your net position?

A Long the underlying forward
B Short the underlying forward
C Long a straddle
D Flat

24. An £ FRN pays a coupon of 20 basis point over LIBOR. The LIBOR is set today at 5.20 %. Does this mean that the FRN will

A Pay a coupon of 5.00% for the period just completed
B Pay a coupon of 5.40% for the period just completed
C Pay a coupon of 5.00% for the period starting today
D Pay a coupon pf 5.40% for the period starting today

25. Which of the following option strategies may be regarded as generally bearish?

    I   Buying a call option
    II   Selling a call option
    III Buying a put option
    IV Selling a put option

A I and II
B I and III
C II and III
D II and IV

26. Who or what is ISDA?

A International Securities Dealers Association
B International Securities Documentation Authority
C International Swaps Documentation Association
D International Swaps and Derivatives Association

27. **Which two of the following swaps are single currency basis swaps?**

    I   6mth v 3 mth USD LIBOR
    II   6% fixed v GBP 3mth LIBOR
    III 6mth USD LIBOR v 3mth GBP LIBOR
    IV   6mth USD LIBOR v 3 mth Treasury Bill rates

    A I and IV
    B II and III
    C I and III
    D II and IV

28. **An up-and-in put option has a 1-month expiry, a strike of 100 and a barrier of 105. The current market price is 100. What is the ideal market scenario for the holder of the option?**

    A The market rises to over 105 at expiry
    B The market rises to 105 then falls below 100 at expiry
    C The market falls significantly
    D The market falls below 100 then finishes at over 105 at expiry

29. **Why might an investor enter into an FRA?**

    A To hedge a credit exposure
    B To hedge against movements in EUR against USD
    C To achieve a cheaper overall cost of finance
    D To reserve the option to fix interest rates at a future date

30. **Which of the following is a correct description of an OIS?**

    A Ordinary Index Swap – a fixed rate of interest is paid in exchange for the return on the FTSE Ordinary All-Share Index
    B Overseas Investment Swap – a type of emerging markets contract for difference
    C OTC Indexation Swap – a composite index of market swap prices in each currency
    D Overnight Index Swap – an exchange of overnight interest rates for a fixed rate

31. **Which of the following is not true of NDFs?**

    A They facilitate trading in inconvertible currencies
    B They reduce settlement risk
    C The buyer need not deliver if the deal is OTM
    D They may be closed out before maturity

32. Which one of the following is one of the uses of yield curves?
    A To determine the maturity of certain issues
    B To determine a forward exchange rate
    C To predict investor interest in bonds
    D To price a corporate bond

33. What is the benefit to a fund manager of being the fixed receiver in an equity or total return swap?
    A The fund's performance is made more predictable
    B It is a yield-enhancement play
    C It is an efficient means of assuming credit risk without having buy the assets
    D Safe custody fees are reduced

34. If a single ATM call option is constructed on a basket of shares, rather than individual ATM call options on each share, which of the following is true?
    A The option seller will be exposed to higher levels of risk
    B The single basket option will be simpler to value
    C The buyer of the basket option pays less total premium
    D The deal must be reported to LIFFE

35. Which two of the following options can be exercised at various opportunities prior to expiry?
    A Bermudan and Asian
    B Asian and American
    C Bermudan and American
    D European and American

36. Which of the following is not a reason why exchange-traded options have grown in volume more substantially than over-the-counter options?
    A Low credit risk
    B Standardised contracts
    C Liquidity
    D Flexibility

37. A bank enters into a vanilla IRS. Which of the following risks to the bank is not increased?
    A Market risk
    B Operational risk
    C Currency risk
    D Credit risk

38. Which of the following is not an occurrence of systems risk?
    A   Computer power outage
    B   Unauthorised access to database
    C   Straight-through processing
    D   Different derivative valuation models in use

39. Which of the following is the best definition of a Forward Rate Agreement?
    A   Option on a forward contract
    B   Contract for a difference that settles on interest rates
    C   Option on a swap contract
    D   Right to buy asset at a fixed price

40. Two banks that regularly deal with each other enter into a currency swap. What new documentation is most likely required?
    A   Regulatory approval
    B   Deal confirmation
    C   Master agreement
    D   Credit agreement

41. What is the benefit to organisations of signing a Master Agreement?
    A   It provides watertight legal protection
    B   It improves relations with ISDA
    C   It simplifies future bilateral dealings
    D   It lessens the probability of default

42. A French bank buys EUR FRA from a German bank with a notional principal of EUR 10m. It has 182 days in the period and settles against a rate of 6%. The contract rate is 5.75%. What is the settlement amount and to whom is it payable?
    A   EUR 12,638.89 owed to French bank
    B   EUR 12,638.89 owed to German bank
    C   EUR 12,226.80 owed to French bank
    D   EUR 12,266.80 owed to German bank

43. A bank has traded a swap as a nominated hedge for a particular exposure. What is the accounting treatment for the swap?
    A   It will be marked-to-market daily
    B   It will appear on both balance sheet and P&L at cost
    C   It will have its P&L calculated over the same period as the underlying
    D   The swap means the underlying exposure can be removed from the balance sheet

44. Which of the following would appear on a bank's balance sheet?
   A   A LIBOR-linked FRN
   B   A LIBOR-linked FRA
   C   A LIBOR-linked vanilla swap with no principal exchange
   D   A LIBOR-linked currency swap with principal exchange

45. A swap which allows the exchange of exposure to correlation for a predetermined strike level is know as a
   A   Commodity swap
   B   Correlation swap
   C   Equity swap
   D   Variance swap

46. Which of the following elements is least likely to influence the organisation of the derivatives operations department?
   A   Size of deal
   B   Number of deals
   C   Types of deal
   D   Risk monitoring of deals

47. When is a deal considered to have been executed?
   A   When the dealer/dealer conversation is ended
   B   When the confirmations have been exchanged and agreed
   C   When the key elements of the deal have been agreed
   D   When the Master Agreement comes into force

48. For settlement purposes, which of the following products requires most frequent reference to market rates?
   A   Barrier option
   B   Interest rate cap
   C   Asian option
   D   Currency swap

49. What is a 'haircut'?
   A   Asking for further margin
   B   The change in the value of collateral
   C   The excess value of collateral over risk
   D   The net balance of mutual collateral that two parties have exchanged

50. Which of the following initiatives in the OTC market is not aimed at risk reduction?
    A   Use of Master Agreements
    B   Use of netting agreements
    C   Use of clearing organisations
    D   Use of third-party organisations for administration

Answers

1. **A**

   See Workbook, Chapter 1

2. **D** Some forwards, such as index forwards, are always cash settled. With all futures and forwards, delivery may be avoided by closing the position before delivery is due

   See Workbook, Chapter 1

3. **A** Credit problems are resolved through the payment of margin to a clearing house

   See Workbook, Chapter 1

4. **C**

   See Workbook Chapter 1

5. **D** LIBOR is not fixed for all currencies, but it is for euros

   See Workbook, Chapter 3

6. **B** A is true for EURIBOR

   See Workbook, Chapter 3

7. **B** Transacting in cash is pointless

   See Workbook, Chapter 3

8. **C** All other answers would lead A to buy the FRA

   See Workbook, Chapter 3

9. **B** The day count is 31/360 and the settlement difference of 0.5% must be discounted at 3.25%

   See Workbook, Chapter 3

10. **C** The parties' motivations are unknown

    See Workbook, Chapter 3

11. **D**

    Workbook Chapter 2

12. **C** The three-month rate is expected to rise relative to the six-month rate

    See Workbook, Chapters 1 and 3

13. **B** Sterling needs to be fixed to eliminate uncertainty of income. No funding requirement, so no principal payment. The sterling payments are set so that their PV equals that of the USD flows

    See Workbook, Chapter 3

OTC Derivatives ♦ Practice Examination 1 – Answers

14. **D** All months have 30 days, regardless

    See Workbook, Chapter 3

15. **D**

    See Workbook, Chapter 3

16. **D**

    See Workbook, Chapter 2

17. **B**

    See Workbook Chapter 2

18. **B** NPV provides a common denominator stripping out the time value of money element of a future cash flow

    See workbook Chapter 3

19. **C** The option is ITM so is exercised by the holder against the fund manager (4,200 – 4,000) × £1,000 = £200,000 must be paid, offset by £50,000 of premium received

    See Workbook, Chapter 2

20. **D** To calculate breakeven, work in the same units. The trader paid US$25,000, which is 25,000 × 120 = ¥3,000,000, or ¥3.00 per US$ of option. To recover this, he needs to exercise for ¥3.00 per US$ profit, which occurs in this dollar put option at 117.00

    See Workbook, Chapter 6

21. **A** Higher volatility expectation means higher potential profits from the option and thus higher value

    See Workbook, Chapter 1

22. **D** II and III would imply a sale of the bond option. IV will lead to I

    See Workbook, Chapter 2

23. **B** Whichever option is exercised (it won't be both), you will sell the underlying on the expiry date

    See Workbook, Chapter 3

24. **D** The FRN re-set refers to the ensuing coupon, and is priced at the LIBOR plus the margin

    See Workbook, Chapter 3

25. **C**

    See Workbook, Chapter 2

26. **D**

    See Workbook, Chapter 7

27. **A** A floating/floating swap is a basis swap. Single currency means that both legs of the swap are in the same currency as opposed to a cross-currency basis swap

    See Workbook Chapter 3

OTC Derivatives ♦ Practice Examination 1 – Answers

28. B   The option will only become active if the barrier is breached; after that it behaves like a vanilla option

   See Workbook, Chapter 2

29. C   This is the most appropriate. The wording in A may be tempting but credit exposure is the main consideration when looking at outstanding payment due in the event of counterparty default

   See Workbook, Chapter 3

30. D

   See Workbook, Chapter 3

31. C   There is no optionality in a non-deliverable forward

   See Workbook, Chapter 6

32. D   The yield curve provides a useful tool for comparing fixed income instruments across different markets and, in particular, for determining spreads for corporate bonds

   See Workbook Chapter 1

33. A   The uncertain performance of the asset is exchanged for a known cash flow

   See Workbook, Chapter 5

34. C   Not discussed in the workbook but is mentioned in syllabus element 4.6.4 A basket's total value volatility will be reduced when correlation is not perfect so the option will be cheap. Individual options permit 'cherry picking' of ITM outcomes

   See Workbook, Chapter 5

35. C   A Bermudan-style option usually has a number of potential dates when it can be exercised. An American-style option can be exercised at any time up to and including expiry

   See Workbook, Chapter 2

36. D

   See Workbook, Chapter 1

37. C   IRS is single-currency deal so no FX risk

   See Workbook, Chapter 1

38. C   STP is a desirable process to minimise error and improve efficiency

   See Workbook, Chapters 1 and 7

39. B

   See Workbook, Chapter 3

40. B   A and D are not required; C should already be in place

   See Workbook, Chapter 7

41. C

    See Workbook, Chapter 7

42. C The French bank buys the FRA therefore is paying fixed at the contract rate of 5.75%. The German bank will, therefore, owe the French bank

    $$\frac{EUR\ 10m \times 0.0025 \times 182/360}{1+(0.06 \times 182/360)} = EUR\ 12,266.80$$

    See Workbook, Chapter 3

43. C

    See Workbook, Chapter 1

44. A A Floating Rate Note is a real asset and must be shown, either as an asset if bought or as a liability if issued

    See Workbook, Chapter 1

45. B

    See Workbook Chapter 5

46. A Processes are the same no matter the amount on the ticket

    See Workbook, Chapter 7

47. C The dealers could continue talking after the deal is considered done

    See Workbook, Chapter 7

48. A The barrier option requires constant monitoring, the others regular fixings only

    See Workbook, Chapter 7

49. C

    See Workbook, Chapter 1

50. A

    See Workbook, Chapter 1

Practice Examination 2

50 Questions in 1 Hour

1. **Which of the following is the best definition of a forward contract?**

    A An agreement between two counterparties to pay each other profits and losses as market prices change, according to whether they are the buyer or the seller

    B A contract on an exchange where the buyer has the right to take delivery of a standardised lot of the underlying asset at an agreed price up to the specified date in the future

    C A contract between two counterparties where they agree to do a specified deal in the future at a price agreed today

    D A standardised exchange-traded contract where the seller agrees to deliver a specified underlying at an agreed date in the future, and the buyer agrees to take delivery of the same, at a price which is agreed when the deal is done

2. **Futures and forwards are similar in which respects?**

    I   Both are derivatives which may be traded on exchanges

    II   Both provide a means for hedgers to manage their risks

    III Both allow their users to know what future market prices are going to be

    IV Both may be used by arbitrageurs

    A I and II

    B I, II and IV

    C II and IV

    D I, II, III and IV

3. **Which of the following is least relevant when contrasting a Short Term Interest Rate (STIR) future and an FRA covering the same period at the same effective rate?**

    A Margin payments

    B Counterparty risk

    C Settlement risk

    D Interest rate sensitivity

4. **A company borrows for a period of five years. The interest rate it pays the bank is fixed for a three-month period, then reset for each subsequent three-month period. What is the arrangement called?**

    A A fixed-rate loan

    B A floating-rate loan

    C A fixed/floating rate loan

    D A fixed/floating rate swap

5. How do EURIBOR and euro LIBOR differ?

    I   EURIBOR is compiled from a wider panel of banks
    II   Euro LIBOR compilation is restricted to British banks only
    III EURIBOR is published to three decimal places; LIBOR to five
    IV   EURIBOR is published earlier in the day

    A I and III
    B II and IV
    C I, III and IV
    D I, II, II and IV

6. What is unique about sterling LIBOR among other LIBOR rates?

    A It includes stamp duty
    B It includes fixings for short-date periods
    C Only British banks contribute to the calculation
    D It is for same-day value

7. When is the principal amount of a euro-denominated FRA settled?

    A Two business days after the fixing
    B When the FRA rate is agreed
    C On the termination date
    D Never

8. The buyer of a 1 × 4 US$ FRA at 4% for $2 million (covering a period of 91 days) notes that LIBOR is fixed at 4.25%. What is the settlement?

    A US$ 1,263.89 to pay
    B US$ 1,263.89 to receive
    C US$ 1,250.46 to pay
    D US$ 1,250.46 to receive

9. Interest rate swaps may be defined as

    A Obligations to exchange loan agreements
    B Renegotiations of interest rate obligations
    C Agreements to exchange an interest payment
    D Agreements to pay each other different series of cash flows

10. In an IRS, to what does the calculation period refer?

    A   The time between rate fixing and settlement
    B   The length of the period that the interest calculations are applied to
    C   The duration of the swap
    D   The gap between trade date and the beginning of the first period

11. What is meant by credit arbitrage?

    A   Exploiting timing mismatches in credit payments
    B   Paying one rate in one IRS and receiving a better rate in another
    C   Exploiting the different relative borrowing strength in different markets to raise finance more efficiently
    D   Borrowing from a high quality name and lending to a poor name at higher rates

12. A bank has a large number of investors who leave their funds on overnight deposit, renewed automatically each day. Most of the bank's lending, however, is to companies on a 3-month rollover. Which of the following would best hedge the bank's risk?

    A   Being the payer in an OIS
    B   Being the receiver in an OIS
    C   Being the payer in an IRS against 3-month LIBOR
    D   Being the receiver in an IRS against 3-month LIBOR

13. Which of the following are true of both FRA and IRS contracts?

    I   They are contracts for difference
    II   They are multi-period deals
    III   They incur counterparty credit risk
    IV   Settlement is made after a discounting adjustment

    A   I and II
    B   II and III
    C   III and IV
    D   I and III

14. What factors contribute to a given level of interest rates?

    I   Central bank policy
    II   The cost of liquidity
    III   Inflation rates
    IV   Supply and demand

    A   I and II
    B   II, III and IV
    C   II and IV
    D   I, III and IV

15. All of the following form part of the risk-weighting of assets, except
    A   Counterparty risk
    B   Settlement risk
    C   Large exposure risk
    D   Processing risk

16. The market level is 260. Which of the following options would be described as ITM?
    I   A put option with a strike of 245
    II   A put option with a strike of 275
    III A call option with a strike of 245
    IV   A call option with a strike of 275
    A   I and III
    B   I and IV
    C   II and III
    D   II and IV

17. What are the major differences between an IRS and a currency swap?
    A   The currency swap always has an exchange of principal at the final exchange of payments
    B   The currency swap can be fixed against fixed, whereas the IRS is nearly always fixed floating
    C   The currency swap has greater credit risk
    D   All of the above

18. Which of the following is false with regard to Asian options?
    A   They are cheaper than the comparable European option
    B   The option's payoff is determined by the difference between its strike and an average rate calculated in an agreed fashion
    C   The Asian effect may result in the holder paying the writer upon exercise
    D   Asian options are suitable hedging tools for small but regular cash flows

19. An OTC American style 1-month put option on a UK Gilt is bought. The strike is 97.50 and the bond's current market price is 98.00. Which of the following is correct?
    A   The option has no intrinsic value
    B   The option has no time value
    C   The option will not be worth exercising
    D   The option is ITM

20. An ATM bond option struck at par is valued at 2.50 with a week until maturity. If the bond market and all other factors remain unchanged over the next 24hrs, which of the following is true?

    A   The option's value will increase
    B   The option's value will decrease
    C   The option's value will remain unchanged
    D   Not enough information is given

21. An option is priced at 50, based on a volatility of 10%. All other things constant, if volatility rises to 11%, what will happen to the option's value?

    A   The option's value will increase to 55
    B   The option's value will increase to 51
    C   The option's value will remain unchanged
    D   Not enough information is provided

22. A commodity trader has sold some coffee futures and notes that the long range weather forecast is beginning to look poor for the crop. Which option trades would make his position worse?

    I   Buying a coffee call option
    II   Selling a coffee call option
    III Buying a coffee put option
    IV   Selling a coffee put option

    A   I and III
    B   II and IV
    C   I and IV
    D   II and III

23. If you buy a call option and buy a put option on the same underlying, with the same maturity and with the same strike, what is your net position?

    A   Long the underlying forward
    B   Short the underlying forward
    C   Long a straddle
    D   Flat

24. A trader is long an ATM gold straddle strike 420 at a premium of 20. At expiry the market is trading at 430. What action must the trader take and what is the overall result?

    A   No action, profit 20
    B   Exercise the call, profit 10
    C   Exercise the straddle, profit 10
    D   Exercise the call, loss 10

25. **Which of the following can be used to mitigate credit risk?**

    A The application of key risk indicators

    B Applying appropriate haircuts, allied with daily mark to market margining

    C Focus workshops

    D Benchmarking

26. **Buying a call option with a low strike and selling a call option of the same maturity but with a higher strike could not be described as**

    A A bear spread

    B A call spread

    C A bull spread

    D A strike spread

27. **Which of the following are methods of mitigating operational risk?**

    A Reducing the likelihood of the risk occurring

    B Avoiding the risk

    C Transferring the risk

    D All of the above

28. **What is the effect for a lender of selling a cap?**

    A The loans will earn more interest

    B The balance sheet assets are reduced

    C Overall portfolio interest earnings are protected

    D Overall portfolio interest earnings have an upper limit

29. The USD six month rates are set as follows

    LIBOR   5.25%
    LIMEAN   5.1875%
    LIBID   5.125%

    A trader who originally bought an FRA at 4.75% will

    A Receive the value of 0.375%

    B Receive the value of 0.50%

    C Receive the value of 0.4375%

    D Receive the discounted value of 0.50%

30. **Which of the following concerning the FX forward market is false?**

    A A forward rate is fixed and the deal carries no risk

    B The forward rate is the equilibrium market price between buyers and sellers

    C The forward rate is a mathematical derivative of the spot price and the two relevant interest rates

    D A forward deal may involve cash settlement rather than an exchange of currencies

31. The normal purpose of an asset swap is
    A To exchange one asset for another
    B To make a specific asset's cash flow suit an investor's needs
    C To have the right to deliver an asset for a fixed price
    D To reduce the asset's credit risk

32. A bank has lent $20 million to a company for two years but becomes concerned about the company's credit status. It decides that a credit default swap is the preferred hedge. Which terms need to be negotiated?
    I   Default events
    II   Fixed rate payments
    III Company's dividend policy
    IV   Contingent compensation
    A I, II and IV
    B II and IV
    C II, III and IV
    D I, II, III and IV

33. Which of the following would not be classified as an equity swap?
    A Paying all dividends on ABC Ltd for three years in exchange for those of XYZ Ltd
    B Paying the return of the FTSE 100 index and receiving that of the DAX
    C Selling shares in ABC Ltd for delivery in one year, receiving shares in XYZ Ltd
    D Paying a fixed rate of interest and receiving the dividends of ABC Ltd

34. Why might a commodity swap be more attractive to a hedger than a series of futures contracts?
    I   The swap has lower dealing costs
    II   The swap is dealt with a single counterparty
    III The swap price is constant for all periods
    IV   The swap market may extend beyond the furthest available future
    A I, III and IV
    B I and II
    C II, III and IV
    D III and IV

35. Two securities of the same maturity and from the same issuer both carry a 5% coupon and are both priced at 96.50. An investor notices that the bank offering them is quoting the yield on one to be slightly higher than that on the other. What is the most likely explanation for the difference?
    A The bank is rounding the number differently
    B The bank is more keen to sell that security
    C The coupon is paid more frequently
    D The risk is greater

36. **Interpolation would be used for which of the following?**
   A Arbitrage
   B Buying the near-dated and selling the far-dated future
   C Stub periods
   D Out-of-the-money options

37. **An IRS dealer forgets to hedge a swap where he is paying fixed. Risk control department fail to identify the position. When finally the error is discovered, swap rates have risen. Which of the following is true?**
   A There was no risk as the trader has made a profit
   B The bank was exposed to market risk and operational risk
   C The bank made a loss because of market and operational risk
   D The hedge can be completed retrospectively

38. **Legal risk would not include which of the following?**
   A Bank undertaking illegal transactions
   B Customer suing the bank for personal injury
   C ISDA document unenforceable in relevant jurisdiction
   D Money laundering

39. **Theta describes**
   A The change in the value of an option given a change in volatility
   B The change in the delta of an option given the change in the underlying
   C The change in the value of an option given a reduction in time
   D The change in the value of an option given a change in interest rates

40. **Which ISDA Master Agreement is currently in widest use?**
   A 1987
   B 1992
   C 1995
   D 2000

41. **What is the difference between a 'termination event' and an 'event of default'?**
   A A termination event brings the deal to an end
   B A termination event is an external event under neither parties' control
   C A termination event covers market activity only
   D A termination event results in a payment to the affected party

42. Which of the following is an example of a synthetic FRN?

    A   Buying a fixed coupon bond and selling a fixed for floating swap
    B   Buying a fixed coupon bond and selling a floating for fixed swap
    C   Buying a floating rate note and buying a FRA
    D   Selling a fixed coupon bond and buying a FRA

43. Which of the following are required for a derivative to qualify for hedge accounting?

    I   The derivative should be intended as a hedge
    II   The derivative is subject to ISDA documentation
    III   The underlying transaction should have a reasonable chance of happening (if not already done)
    IV   The derivative is held for at least one month

    A   I and III
    B   I, II and III
    C   II and IV
    D   II, III and IV

44. Which of the following is not considered to be a corporate action?

    A   Buying a share
    B   Payment of a dividend
    C   Issuing of bonus shares
    D   A stock split

45. Which of the following types of swap focuses on volatility?

    A   Dividend swap
    B   Variance swap
    C   Correlation swap
    D   Total return swap

46. What is the most likely sequence of the following post-trade events?

    I   Settlement
    II   Confirmation checking
    III   Collateral update
    IV   Position update

    A   I, II, III, IV
    B   IV, II, III, I
    C   III, IV, I, II
    D   II, III, IV, I

47. Which of the following makes trade capture for options more complex?

   A It is not known whether the option will be exercised
   B The buyer and the seller of the option have asymmetrical risks
   C The premium payment must be reconciled
   D Two levels of trade data are required

48. All other thing being equal, which of the following products requires the highest number of settlement payments?

   A Barrier option
   B Interest rate cap
   C Asian option
   D Currency swap

49. A bank has provided collateral relating to an IRS in which it is the receiver. At the next reset date, swap rates are higher. What happens to the collateral?

   A It is unaffected
   B The bank must provide more collateral
   C The bank will receive a return of some collateral
   D Not enough information is provided

50. Which of the following statements about SwapClear are true?

   I   It is owned and run by LCH
   II   It will act as central counterparty for swaps deals
   III It will act as central counterparty for FRA deals
   IV   Only NYSE Liffe members may be SwapClear Clearing Members

   A I and II
   B I, II and III
   C I, II III and IV
   D II and III

OTC Derivatives ◆ Practice Examination 2 – Answers

Answers

1. **C**   B is an option, D is a future and C is the **best** definition

   See Workbook, Chapter 1

2. **C**   III is impossible for anyone to know

   See Workbook, Chapter 1

3. **D**   The two will have equivalent P&L performance for a given rate movement

   See Workbook, Chapter 3

4. **B**   It would be described as fixed rate only if it were so for the entire period

   See Workbook, Chapter 3

5. **C**   LIBOR is from banks in London, not British banks

   See Workbook, Chapter 3

6. **D**   Other LIBORs are effective T + 2

   See Workbook, Chapter 3

7. **D**   FRAs are contracts for difference only

   See Workbook, Chapter 3

8. **D**   The fixing is higher than the FRA rate so the buyer is to receive the difference; the amount must be discounted

   $$\frac{\$2m \times 0.0025 \times 91/360}{1 + (0.0425 \times 91/360)} = 1{,}250.46$$

   See Workbook, Chapter 3

9. **D**

   See Workbook, Chapter 3

10. **B**

    See Workbook, Chapter 3

11. **C**

    See Workbook, Chapter 4

12. **A**   Overnight Index Swap. The bank is paying variable overnight rates so in the swap should receive them and pay fixed instead; the latter will match its lending income

    See Workbook, Chapter 3

13. **D**

    See Workbook, Chapter 3

OTC Derivatives ♦ Practice Examination 2 – Answers

14. **D** — II is not a contributing factor to interest rates, but another description of what an interest rate is

    See Workbook, Chapter 1

15. **D** — Risk-weighted assets are the total of counterparty risk, settlement risk, position risk, currency and large exposure risk

    See Workbook, Chapter 1

16. **C** — ITM = In-the-money; the strike is better than market for the holder

    See Workbook, Chapter 2

17. **D**

    See Workbook Chapter 3

18. **C** — No option holder would rationally exercise for loss

    See Workbook, Chapter 2

19. **A** — The option is currently OTM with no intrinsic value but need not remain so. It might be worth exercising at some point and hence has some time value

    See Workbook, Chapter 2

20. **B** — An ATM option has no intrinsic value so the premium must all be time value, reflecting the possibility that the market will move in the holder's favour. As time available until expiry decreases, this potential becomes less valuable and so the option decays in value

    See Workbook, Chapter 2

21. **D** — Higher volatility expectation means higher potential profits from the option and thus higher time value, but the link is not direct and we need more information to establish the new price

    See Workbook, Chapter 2

22. **D** — II and III would lose money if the coffee price rises. His underlying futures position is already that way round so the options would merely add to losses

    See Workbook, Chapters 2 and 6

23. **C**

    See Workbook, Chapter 2

24. **D** — Only the call is ITM and worth exercising. It will generate a 10 profit but the 20 spent on premium means net 10 loss

    See Workbook, Chapter 2

25. **B** — Only the application of a haircut to the level of collateral held has anything to do with credit risk management

    See Workbook, Chapter 1

OTC Derivatives ♦ Practice Examination 2 – Answers

26. **A**

    See Workbook, Chapter 2

27. **D** All are valid methods of risk reduction

    See Workbook, Chapters 1 and 7

28. **D** Selling the cap surrenders the benefit of rates rising higher than the cap strike rate

    See Workbook, Chapters 2 and 3

29. **D** The trader receives the difference between the LIBOR, and the traded rate on a discounted basis

    See Workbook, Chapter 3

30. **A** There is no rate risk, but there is counterparty and settlement risk

    See Workbook, Chapter 6

31. **B**

    See Workbook, Chapter 6

32. **A** The company's dividend policy is outside the control of the swap parties

    See Workbook, Chapter 4

33. **C** Answer C is a single exchange and would be classified as a forward

    See Workbook, Chapter 5

34. **D** I is not true; documentation and capital adequacy impact may be costly. II is true also of futures, where the clearing house is the sole counterparty

    See Workbook, Chapter 6

35. **C** More frequent payment means earlier average cash flows and more reinvestment earnings

    See Workbook, Chapter 1

36. **C** Within a swap there may be an irregular length period at the beginning or the end called a stub period or broken period

    See Workbook, Chapter 3

37. **B** The profit outcome was lucky but irrelevant; the bank was exposed

    See Workbook, Chapters 1 and 3

38. **B** This is due legal process rather than legal risk as such

    See Workbook, Chapter 1

39. **C**

    See Workbook Chapter 2

40.	B	
		See Workbook, Chapter 7
41.	B	
		See Workbook, Chapters 4 and 7
42.	A	The fixed coupon would be swapped for a floating coupon, under a pay-fixed swap. You will be selling the fixed leg in exchange for the floating
		See Workbook, Chapters 3 and 6
43.	A	
		See Workbook, Chapter 1
44.	A	Buying and selling a share are not classed as corporate actions
		See Workbook Chapter 5
45.	B	A variance swap allows hedging or speculation of risk associated to the degree of movement in prices or rates
		See Workbook Chapter 5
46.	B	IV must be done immediately
		See Workbook, Chapter 7
47.	D	All are true but only D affects trade capture
		See Workbook, Chapter 7
48.	D	The options settle once maximum, the currency swap requires two payments each settlement date
		See Workbook, Chapter 7
49.	D	Although the mark-to-market of the swap is showing a loss (and you might be tempted to answer B), the collateral itself must also be revalued to determine any change required
		See Workbook, Chapters 1 and 3
50.	B	LCH not LIFFE, is the relevant membership
		See Workbook, Chapter 7

Practice Examination 3

50 Questions in 1 Hour

1. Which of the following is not available as a type of forward contract?

    A   Commodities

    B   Loans

    C   Metals

    D   Energy

2. Which of the following may be traded OTC?

    I   FRAs

    II   Equity index options

    III Interest rate swaps

    IV   Bond futures

    A   I and II

    B   I and III

    C   II, III and IV

    D   I, II and III

3. A travel company specialising in Dubai luxury holidays earns pounds Sterling from its customers and incurs local currency expenses. Which of the following is correct?

    A   The company's FX exposure is too small to be of concern

    B   The company's FX exposure is best covered with a futures contract

    C   The company's FX exposure is best covered with OTC forwards and/or options

    D   The company's FX exposure should not be covered because it is seasonal

4. Derivatives can be used to change the risk profile of traders' portfolios. Can they be applied to

    A   Existing cash exposures

    B   New cash exposures

    C   Existing derivatives

    D   Any of the above

5. Which rate is the main international benchmark for USD interest rates?

    A   USD LIBOR

    B   USD EURIBOR

    C   USD prime rate

    D   USD Fed funds rate

6. **Which of the following statements about an FRA contains no errors?**
   A An FRA is a cash-settled forward contract on an interest rate
   B An FRA is an agreement to pay or receive an agreed fixed interest rate on a loan or borrowing over a future period
   C An FRA is the OTC equivalent of a STIR future and buying either will achieve the same effect
   D An FRA is a tailormade way of managing exchange risk

7. **A buys an FRA from B at 5%. The fixing is 6%. Which of the following payments will be made?**
   A A pays B interest at 5% and receives interest at 6%
   B B pays A interest at 5% and receives interest at 6%
   C A pays B interest at 1%
   D B pays A interest at 1%

8. **A Sterling 3 × 9 FRA for £20 million traded at 5% has its relevant fixing at 4.5% for 181 days. What settlement amount is due?**
   A £48,506.61
   B £49,165.41
   C £49,589.04
   D £50,277.78

9. **Rho describes**
   A The change in the value of an option given a change in volatility
   B The change in the delta of an option given the change in the underlying
   C The change in the value of an option given a reduction in time
   D The change in the value of an option given a change in interest rates

10. **A speculator believes that over the coming month the 5-year swap rate will go down. Which trade would be appropriate?**
    A Selling a 5-year FRA
    B Buying a monthly basis swap
    C Entering a swap as a receiver
    D Entering a swap as a payer

11. **Which of the following is not an example of a basis swap?**
    A Paying 3-month LIBOR and receiving 3-month fixed rate
    B Paying 3-month LIBOR and receiving 6-month LIBOR
    C Paying 3-month sterling LIBOR and receiving 3-month euro LIBOR
    D Paying 3-month LIBOR and receiving base rate

12. **Which of the following concerning a currency swap is false?**
    A A full exchange of cash flows in different currencies is made
    B The principal amount is exchanged
    C One party to the swap may expect all his interest payments to be greater in value than all those he receives
    D Cash flows on the same date will be netted

13. **In a swap, what is the significance of the effective date?**
    A It is the date by which the contract must be cancelled if you do not want to proceed
    B It is the date on which the effective rate is set for each calculation period
    C It is the date on which the Master Agreement is signed
    D It is the date from which the interest calculations begin

14. A vanilla swap has a stub period of 37 days. The LIBOR fixings are

    1 week (7 days)   4.5%

    1 month (30 days) 5.00%

    2 months (61 days) 5.25%

    What rate should be used for the stub period settlement?
    A 9.5%
    B 5.00%
    C 5.125%
    D 5.056%

15. **What is the difference between a forward contract and an OTC option contract?**
    A An option contract does not require the underlying deal to be completed
    B An option contract's underlying deal will take place at a price unknown at the outset
    C An option contract may be sold on to a third party
    D An option contract has no settlement risk

16. **Kappa describes**
    A The change in the value of an option given a change in volatility
    B The change in the delta of an option given the change in the underlying
    C The change in the value of an option given a reduction in time
    D The change in the value of an option given a change in interest rates

17. If an option contract provides for CFD cash settlement on exercise, which of the following are correct?

    I   Physical delivery must be made for cash payment
    II Premium payment occurs when the option is exercised
    III The holder receives the difference between the strike and a reference price
    IV Settlement risk is reduced

    A I and II
    B II and III
    C III and IV
    D I and IV

18. A 6-month Asian sterling call / US$ put option for £1 million is expiring. Its strike is 1.50. The monthly reference rates are 1.4850, 1.4920, 1.5150, 1.5250, 1.4950 and 1.5000. What is the settlement amount?

    A Nil
    B £2,000
    C £2,000
    D £1,500,000

19. A call option has a strike of 120.50 and is valued at 5.00. The underlying market is trading at 124.25. What is the option's time value?

    A Nil
    B 5.00
    C 3.75
    D 1.25

20. What is time decay with respect to an option?

    A The approach of the expiry date
    B The delay between requesting a price and getting it from the market maker
    C The shrinking of the volatility value as time passes
    D The loss in value for a put as the market moves up, or loss for a call as the market moves down over time

21. Which of the following will be the best guide to a potential change in delta, is the price of the underlying changes?

    A Gamma
    B Theta
    C Kappa/Vega
    D Rho

22. **If you buy a call option and sell a put option on the same underlying, with the same maturity and with the same strike, what is your net position?**

    A Long the underlying forward
    B Short the underlying forward
    C Long a straddle
    D Flat

23. **How do you take on a short straddle position?**

    A Buy the call and sell the put with the same strike
    B Buy the short dated call and sell the long-dated call with the same strike
    C Sell the call and sell the put with the same strike
    D Buy the call and sell twice the amount of puts with the same strike

24. **Which of the following is likely to present the greatest potential credit risk, when comparing products of the same notional principle amounts?**

    A FRA
    B IRS
    C OIS
    D Currency swap

25. **If long-term interest rates fall significantly which of the following strategies provides a bond fund manager with the best overall result?**

    A Selling the bond forward
    B A long bond put option position
    C A short bond call option position
    D Remaining unhedged

26. **The swapping of an equity cash flow for equity capital participation, is know as a**

    A Dividend swap
    B Capital swap
    C Interest rate swap
    D Total return swap

27. **A down-and-out call option has a 1-month expiry, a strike of 100 and a barrier of 95. The current market price is 96. Which of the following statements is false?**

    A The option will expire worthless
    B The option is cheaper than if it had no barrier
    C The seller hopes for a fall in the market
    D The option has unlimited profit potential

28. Which of the following combinations may be referred to as a collar?
    - I   Buy a floor and buy a cap
    - II Buy a floor and sell a cap
    - III Sell a floor and buy a cap
    - IV Sell a floor and sell a cap

    A I and IV
    B II and III
    C I, II, III and IV
    D None of the above

29. The holder of a one-month receiver's swaption with a strike of 5% for three years would exercise it under which of the following circumstances?

    A Three-year interest rates have risen higher than market expectations
    B Three-year swap rates are less than 5%
    C LIBOR rates appear low and are expected to rise
    D He needs to fix his interest rate expense for the next three years

30. A currency speculator believes that the dollar is going to strengthen quite strongly. The current sterling/dollar rate is 1.5000. Which of the following trades makes most sense?

    A Buy a sterling call strike 1.5500
    B Buy a sterling call, strike 1.4500
    C Buy a sterling put, strike 1.5500
    D Buy a sterling put, strike 1.4500

31. A bank's bond salesperson wants to use a swap to sell a five-year FRN to an investor who usually buys only fixed-rate paper. Which of the following is least relevant to achieving the sale?

    A The credit rating of the issuer
    B The credit rating of the bank
    C The FRN coupon frequency
    D The five-year swap rate

32. A credit spread option is best defined as

    A An option giving the holder the right to sell one bond and buy another
    B An option on a credit default swap
    C An option spread that generates net premium income
    D An option whose strike is the yield difference between that of a named bond and a reference rate

33. Trading in derivatives based on an equity index such as the FTSE 100 is characterised by which of the following?

   A Traders are always bound by the rules of the stock exchange
   B The derivatives are cash-settled
   C Company dividends have no effect on the index
   D The index constituents are stable in the long term

34. A speculator in precious metals believes that over the next two years, the price of gold relative to the price of silver will increase. What swap structure would profit from this view being correct?

   A Receiving fixed silver, paying floating gold
   B Paying fixed silver, receiving floating gold
   C Paying fixed gold, receiving floating silver
   D Receiving floating gold, paying floating silver

35. An investor buys a four-year zero coupon bond at a yield of 6% p.a. What price does he pay for the bond?

   A 76.00
   B 79.21
   C 94.00
   D 98.74

36. A borrower issues commercial paper for value 13 July with a face amount of €5 million to be redeemed on 13 August. The buyer's yield is 4.5% p.a. What is the price of the CP?

   A €4,980,700
   B €4,980,963
   C €4,981,320
   D €4,981,575

37. Which of the following trades carries the least credit risk, assuming the counterparty and size of deal is the same in each case?

   A Selling a 6 × 12 FRA
   B Selling a 5-year interest rate swap
   C Selling a 5-year currency swap
   D Selling a 5-year currency option

38. Which of the following give rise to operational risk?
   - I   Trade data input
   - II SSI database maintenance
   - III Changes in market volatility
   - IV Expiry of OTM options

   A   I and II
   B   II and III
   C   III and IV
   D   I and IV

39. An exchange of payments in different currencies over a period of time is a
   A   Currency swap
   B   Currency forward
   C   Equity swap
   D   Commodity swap

40. The ISDA Master Agreement covers which of the following?
   A   Contract currency
   B   Tax indemnities
   C   Assignment
   D   All the above

41. If both parties are affected by a termination event, how is the closing settlement amount decided?
   A   It is calculated by ISDA
   B   It is referred to an arbitrator
   C   It is the average of the two figures calculated by the parties
   D   It is the sum required by the party suffering a loss

42. In which year were the ISDA FX and currency option definitions published?
   A   1992
   B   1994
   C   1996
   D   1998

43. US dollar LIBOR is set at
   A   Two days before start date
   B   Two days after settlement date
   C   On settlement date
   D   On trade date

44. In which of the following situations would the equity derivative cease trading
    A Low liquidity
    B High volatility
    C Suspension of the underlying share in the cash market
    D Pending an FSA investigation into a company

45. If you are moderately bearish, and decide to sell a low strike put option, and buy a high strike put option, what have you created?
    A A long put spread
    B A short put spread
    C A long straddle
    D A short strangle

46. Which of the following are advantages of STP?
    I   Lower deal administration costs
    II   Exception-based reporting
    III Improved deal capture
    IV   Product simplification
    A I, II, III, and IV
    B I, III and IV
    C III and IV
    D I and II

47. Which of the following are objectives of trade verification?
    I   To check that the deal was traded on a business day
    II   To check that the deal is booked at market rates
    III To check that the deal is suitable for the counterparty market maker
    IV   To check that the deal breached no internal limits
    A I, II, III and IV
    B II, III and IV
    C II and IV
    D I and III

48. With what should the Nostro ledger be reconciled?
    A The payments that have been made and received
    B The Nostro account
    C The account-holding bank's statement
    D The dealer's position

49. Which of the following is not a potential benefit of setting up SSIs?
    A   Reduces number of settlement payments
    B   Help prevent money laundering
    C   Enhances benefits of STP
    D   Saves the dealer time

50. The Japanese day count for international money market transactions is
    A   Actual/365
    B   Actual/360
    C   Actual/Actual
    D   30E/360

Answers

1. **B** Loans are a cash product
   See Workbook, Chapter 1

2. **D** Futures are by definition exchange-traded
   See Workbook, Chapter 1

3. **C** UAE dirhams are a minor currency, not available as a listed futures contract
   See Workbook, Chapter 6

4. **D** Derivatives are incredibly flexible
   See Workbook, Chapter 1

5. **A** B doesn't exist; C and D are primarily domestic
   See Workbook, Chapter 3

6. **A** FRAs are interest-rate CFDs and the buy/sell sense is opposite to that of futures
   See Workbook, Chapter 3

7. **D** The buyer benefits from the higher LIBOR fixing and answer A is part of the calculation but the settlement is netted, so D is correct
   See Workbook, Chapter 3

8. **A** Sterling is Act/365 and the amount must be discounted
   See Workbook, Chapter 3

9. **D** Rho reflects interest rate changes
   See Workbook, Chapter 2

10. **C** Payer/receiver refer to the fixed rate leg. Once rates have fallen, he could enter a new swap pay at a lower rate to square out and take profit
    See Workbook, Chapter 3

11. **A** A is a simple vanilla swap
    See Workbook, Chapter 3

12. **D** No netting is not possible as flows are in different currencies
    See Workbook, Chapter 3

13. **D**
    See Workbook, Chapter 3

14. **D** $[(0.0525 - 0.05)/(61 - 30) \times 7] + 0.05 = 0.05056$, i.e. 5.056%
    See Workbook, Chapter 3

OTC Derivatives ♦ Practice Examination 3 – Answers

15. A   All other statements are untrue

   See Workbook, Chapters 1 and 3

16. A   Kappa, also known as Vega reflects the changing value of the option due to changes in volatility

   See Workbook, Chapter 2

17. C   Contracts for differences result in net cash settlement, option holder will receive this. Smaller payments reduce risk

   See Workbook, Chapter 2

18. C   The average of the reference rates is US$ 1.5020. The option gives the right to buy sterling at US$ 1.5000 so it is ITM and the difference of US$ 0.0020 per sterling is due to the holder. The option is for £1,000,000 giving 1,000,000 × US$ 0.0020 = US$ 2,000

   See Workbook, Chapter 2

19. D   Time value = Premium – Intrinsic value, giving 5.00 – (124.25 – 120.50) = 1.25

   See Workbook, Chapter 2

20. C   Time value in an option depends on market volatility and remaining time to expiry available, thus also known as volatility value. Less time means less opportunity for change

   See Workbook, Chapter 2

21. A   Gamma reflects the change in Delta given the change in the underlying price

   See Workbook, Chapter 2

22. A   Whichever option is exercised (it won't be both), you will own the underlying on the expiry date

   See Workbook, Chapter 2

23. C

   See Workbook, Chapter 2

24. D   Currency swaps are the only one of the choices that exchange principal amounts as well as interest flows

   See Workbook, Chapter 1

25. D   If interest rates fall, bond prices rise. B is wasted money, and A and C sacrifice profits

   See Workbook, Chapters 1 and 3

26. A   B does not exist. A Total Return Swap swaps both income and capital returns

   See Workbook Chapter 5

27. A   The option will only expire worthless if the barrier is breached or if the market is below 100 at expiry. The price could move up and take the option ITM

   See Workbook, Chapter 2

OTC Derivatives ♦ Practice Examination 3 – Questions

28. B   Collars involve buying a protective option and funding it by sacrificing some benefit by selling a complementary option

See Workbook, Chapters 2 and 3

29. B   Like all options, simply compare strike v market and exercise if ITM

See Workbook, Chapters 2 and 3

30. D   The FX rate is USD per GBP; a stronger dollar means lower rates. The speculator needs a USD call, i.e. a GBP put. 1.45 strike is OTM, will be cheaper and provide a better return on investment

See Workbook, Chapter 6

31. C   An asset swap can be structured to pay the investor the fixed rate payments at whatever frequency he desires. The bank's credit quality is relevant for the swap

See Workbook, Chapters 3 and 6

32. D

See Workbook, Chapter 4

33. B   Settling the underlying shares is too onerous

See Workbook, Chapter 5

34. D   The relative price is the focus, not the absolute price

See Workbook, Chapter 6

35. B   Price = 100 / 1.06^4 (if your calculator doesn't have a power function, x^4 is the same as $x^2{}^2$). The answer is in any case the only reasonable one given the numbers; no calculation is necessary

See Workbook, Chapter 3

36. A   This is a simple discounting question which requires you to calculate the present value of €5m

Price = Face Amt / (1 + (0.045 × 31/360)). Day count = Act/360

See Workbook, Chapter 3

37. D   The option has no credit risk (after receipt of premium) as the holder would only exercise for profit

See Workbook, Chapter 1

38. A   Volatility is market risk and OTM options require no action

See Workbook, Chapters 1 and 7

39. A

See Workbook, Chapter 3

40. D

See Workbook, Chapter 7

41. **C**   Termination events are no-fault events with no bias to either party

   See Workbook, Chapter 7

42. **D**

   See Workbook, Chapter 7

43. **A**

   See Workbook, Chapter 3

44. **C**   An equity derivative will cease trading when the underlying share is suspended from trading. Low liquidity may make it more difficult to trade. A company and its shares may continue trading during an investigation, at the discretion of the FSA

   See Workbook Chapter 5

45. **A**   This trade creates a net initial debit (outflow of premium). Hence this is a long position in the put spread

   See Workbook Chapter 2

46. **D**   Deal capture is required under any system; and the product is unaffected (although STP may be unable to cope with the more complex products, which is a different matter)

   See Workbook, Chapter 7

47. **C**   I is unnecessary and III applies only to non-professional counterparties

   See Workbook, Chapter 7

48. **C**   The Nostro ledger is a mirror image of the account held at another bank. Payments generate entries

   See Workbook, Chapter 7

49. **A**   Standing Settlement Instructions are different to netting agreements

   See Workbook, Chapter 7

50. **B**

   See Workbook, Chapter 3